What's the Difference?
Monkeys and Apes

by Lisa M. Herrington

Content Consultant
Dr. Lucy Spelman

Reading Consultant
Jeanne M. Clidas, Ph.D.
Reading Specialist

Children's Press®
An Imprint of Scholastic Inc.

Library of Congress Cataloging-in-Publication Data

Herrington, Lisa M., author.
  Monkeys and apes / by Lisa M. Herrington.
    pages cm. -- (Rookie read-about science. What's the difference)
  Summary: "Introduces the reader to monkeys and apes."-- Provided by publisher.
  ISBN 978-0-531-21486-2 (library binding) -- ISBN 978-0-531-21534-0 (pbk.)
1. Monkeys--Miscellanea--Juvenile literature. 2. Apes--Miscellanea--Juvenile
literature. 3. Children's questions and answers. I. Title.

QL737.P925H47 2016
599.8--dc23   2015017326

Produced by Spooky Cheetah Press
Design by Keith Plechaty

Printed in China 62

SCHOLASTIC, CHILDREN'S PRESS, ROOKIE READ-ABOUT®, and associated logos
are trademarks and/or registered trademarks of Scholastic Inc.

1 2 3 4 5 6 7 8 9 10 R 25 24 23 22 21 20 19 18 17 16

Photographs ©: cover left: Minden Pictures/Superstock, Inc.; cover right: Thomas
Marent/Minden Pictures; 3 left: neuson11/Thinkstock; 3 right: Eric Isselée/Thinkstock;
4 top: Thomas Marent/Minden Pictures; 7 top: Minden Pictures/Superstock, Inc.; 7
bottom: Sohns/imagebroker/Superstock, Inc.; 8: Minden Pictures/Superstock, Inc.;
11: Mint Images/Superstock, Inc.; 12: bluedogroom/Shutterstock, Inc.; 15: Thomas
Marent/Minden Pictures; 16: Animals Animals/Superstock, Inc.; 19: lobaszo/Thinkstock;
20, 23: Minden Pictures/Superstock, Inc.; 24: Anolis01/Thinkstock; 25 top: Anup Shah/
Minden Pictures; 25 center: kjorgen/Thinkstock; 25 bottom, 26: Minden Pictures/
Superstock, Inc.; 28 top: blickwinkel/Alamy Images; 28 bottom: Steve Bloom Images/
Superstock, Inc.; 29 top: Andrew Suryono, courtesy of Sony World Photography
awards 2014/wenn.com/Newscom; 29 bottom: Minden Pictures/Superstock, Inc.;
30: Iredman/Dreamstime; 31 top: Andrew Suryono, courtesy of Sony World
Photography awards 2014/WENN.com/Newscom; 31 center top: Mint Images/
Superstock, Inc.; 31 center bottom, 31 bottom: Minden Pictures/Superstock, Inc.

Map by XNR Productions, Inc.

Table of Contents

4

Which Is Which?

They both have fur. They both have two arms and two legs. They are both **primates** (PRYE-mates).

Most have thumbs that can **grasp** objects. But which is the monkey and which is the ape?

Did you guess right? Monkeys and apes are a lot alike. But they are not exactly the same. There are ways to tell them apart.

Humans are also part of the primate family. Our closest relatives are chimpanzees and bonobos (buh-NO-bohs).

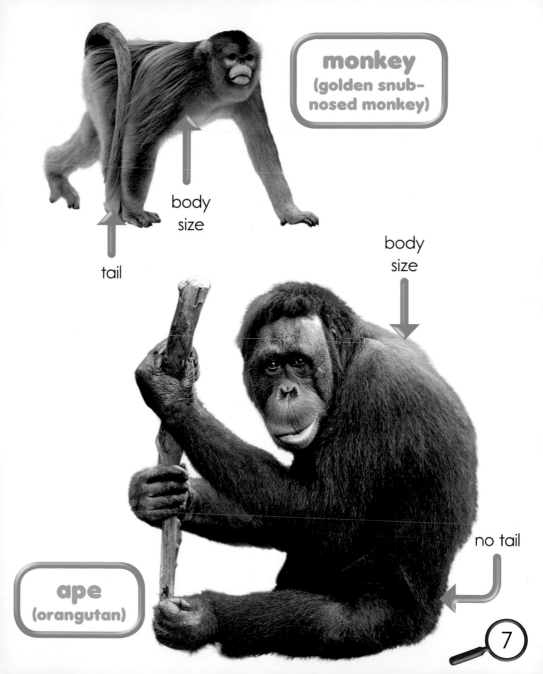

monkey
(golden snub-nosed monkey)

body
size

tail

body
size

no tail

ape
(orangutan)

7

A spider monkey uses its strong tail to hang on to a branch.

Tale of the Tail

What is one way to tell these animals apart? Look at their rear ends!

Most monkeys have a tail. Some have a **prehensile** (pree-HEN-sil) **tail**. That means they can grab, or grasp, things with it. These monkeys use the tail like a fifth arm to help them climb through the trees of their **habitat**. Others have a tail that does not grab things.

9

Apes do not have tails. They use their strong arms and legs to get around.

Most apes have arms that are longer than their legs. They use their arms to swing through trees or walk on all fours. They can also walk on two legs.

Apes lean on their knuckles when walking on all fours. This is called knuckle walking.

orangutan
(uh-RANG-uh-tan)

11

pygmy marmoset

How Big?

Monkeys are mostly smaller than apes.

The world's smallest monkey is the pygmy (PIG-mee) marmoset. It is only about 5 inches (13 centimeters) tall.

The largest monkey is the mandrill. It is about 3 feet (1 meter) tall. That is about the size of a three-year-old child!

Most apes are bigger than monkeys.

Gorillas, chimpanzees, orangutans, and bonobos are called great apes. Gorillas are the largest of the apes. They can grow up to 6 feet (2 meters) tall. That is as tall as many adults!

Gibbons and siamangs (SEE-uh-mangs) are called lesser apes. They can grow to a little more than 2 feet (0.6 meters) tall.

The white-bearded gibbon uses its long arms to swing through the trees in its jungle habitat.

The Nose Knows

Monkeys usually have bigger noses than apes. They count more on their sense of smell than apes do. Monkeys sniff around to find out what other animals have been in the area.

The male proboscis (PRO-bah-sis) monkey has a very large nose.

Apes use their eyes more than their noses. They count on their sense of sight more than their sense of smell.

Their noses look different from monkey noses, too. Apes have flatter, wider noses than monkeys.

FUN FACT!

One big difference between monkeys and apes cannot be seen. Apes are more intelligent than monkeys. They can think and solve problems. They use rocks and sticks as tools to get food.

gorilla

19

Bringing Up Babies

Both monkeys and apes are good parents.

Some monkey mothers stay with their young until they are one or two years old.

This silverly langur baby has orange fur. Its fur will turn gray when it is about five months old.

Apes care for their babies longer than monkeys do. Apes usually have one baby at a time. They spend many years raising their young. Young chimpanzees and orangutans stay with their mothers for about seven years.

Now you know the difference between these animal look-alikes!

A baby gorilla often rides on its mother's back.

Monkeys and Apes

Monkeys live in Africa, Asia and Central and South America.

Apes live in Africa and Asia.

The **golden lion tamarin** is named for the thick golden hair around its face. This monkey lives in South America.

North America
South America
MAP KEY
Ape range
Monkey range

Around the World

Unlike other monkeys, the **mantled colobus** (KOL-uh-bus) **monkey** has no thumbs.

Gibbons, **siamangs**, and orangutans live in Asia.

Europe

Asia

Africa

Gorillas, chimpanzees, and **bonobos** are all great apes that live in Africa.

Australia

usually has a tail

monkey
(spider monkey)

small, light body

26

Howler monkeys are the world's loudest land animals. When a group of them howl together, they can be heard up to 3 miles (5 km) away.

Japanese macaques (muh-KAKS) like to make snowballs and play in the snow.

Amazing!

Orangutans sometimes use leaves to protect themselves from rain.

Chimpanzees put sticks into termite homes, called mounds. The insects crawl up the sticks and the chimps eat them.

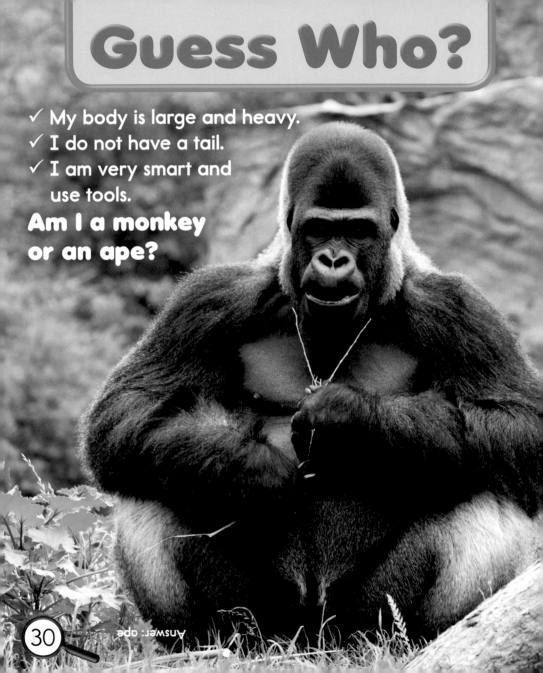

Guess Who?

- ✓ My body is large and heavy.
- ✓ I do not have a tail.
- ✓ I am very smart and use tools.

Am I a monkey or an ape?

Answer: ape

30

Glossary

grasp (GRASP): grab something

habitat (HAB-uh-tat): the kind of place where an animal makes its home

prehensile tail (pree-HEN-sil TAYL): tail that can grab or hold something

primates (PRYE-mates): animal group that includes humans, monkeys, and apes

Index

Facts for Now

Visit this Scholastic Web site for more information
on monkeys and apes:
www.factsfornow.scholastic.com
Enter the keywords **Monkeys and Apes**

About the Author

Lisa M. Herrington loves writing books about animals for kids.
She lives in Trumbull, Connecticut, with her husband, Ryan, and
daughter, Caroline.